CONTENTS

Introduction 2

Chapter 1.   Essential Veterinary Care 4

Chapter 2.   Equipment 6

Chapter 3.   Proper Diet, Food Supplements
             and Treats 10

Chapter 4.   Method 13

Chapter 5.   Schedule 18

Chapter 6.   Misconceptions 22

             Points to Remember 25

INTRODUCTION

Our housebreaking method will result in a puppy or dog that eliminates quickly on command and controls its bodily functions for a reasonable length of time that can exceed eight hours.

Our method is safe and effective for all types and sizes of dogs, from Toys to Giants, Yorkies to Mastiffs, and everything in between.

Our program can be initiated when the puppy is **eight weeks old,** an age at which we have always advocated that training could begin, and now a fact that has been validated by scientific evidence. The method is also proven effective on **older puppies or dogs** of any age.

Our program is suitable for any owner, regardless of your work schedule, lifestyle or whether you live in an apartment or private home.

In developing this method, we have drawn directly from our experiences in working with thousands of dogs of all sizes, breeds and ages, their owners' needs, and the input of practicing veterinarians and scientific data available through veterinary school behavior clinics.

Included in this text is all the pertinent information you will need to successfully housebreak your dog.

---

*Footnote: Use of "he," "his," "him" in this text refers to both male and female dogs and puppies.

CHAPTER 1

ESSENTIAL VETERINARY CARE

Veterinary care is necessary to ensure quick and lasting success with any housebreaking program.

Besides the obvious need for a comprehensive vaccination schedule and preventive medical program, it is important to rule out current medical conditions that may contribute to problems in housebreaking your dog.

The majority of dogs that defecate or urinate in the house do so because they were never properly housebroken in the first place. However, there can be a medical reason for a dog to defecate or urinate inappropriately.

A dog or puppy that is exhibiting more than a normal need to urinate may have cystitis or another urinary tract problem. Intestinal parasites can cause diarrhea, inconsistent stools or a more frequent need to defecate.

As dogs age, senility and incontinence due to decreasing hormonal levels can cause disruptions in housebreaking. Though less common, certain metabolic diseases such as diabetes, can cause dogs or puppies to drink more water and urinate more.

Combined medical and behavioral treatment can help to effect control and management of these conditions.

By taking responsible care of your dog's health you can eliminate medical reasons for housebreaking problems.

CHAPTER 2

EQUIPMENT

Obtaining and utilizing the proper equipment is essential for the successful housebreaking of your dog.

CRATES

Your untrained puppy or dog must be kept in a safe place when left alone.

Our training method has evolved over the years

from confining a puppy or untrained dog in a small bathroom, kitchen or laundry room, to the **safer** and more **practical** use of a crate. Since dogs will try not to soil their sleeping area, the utilization of a crate will help in the housebreaking process. In addition, by keeping your dog or puppy confined in a crate you can also prevent destructive behavior that could result in unnecessary damage, expense and physical harm to your pet.

Crates are not cruel. In fact, they are a safe haven, most comparable to a crib or playpen for an infant or toddler. When used properly, most dogs will find security and comfort in the fact that the crate is "their place."

Whenever possible, keep the crate in an area frequented by the family so that the dog will feel like he is part of the "clan."

Buy a crate that will accommodate and be comfortable for the dog as he grows to physical maturity.

Line the crate with old or inexpensive towels. They are comfortable, absorbent and can be washed and reused. Keep them trimmed to prevent ingestion of any loose threads. Many breeders use newspapers to line their kennel areas. Puppies may have become accustomed to urinating and defecating on them. If used in their crate the puppy may still associate them with this purpose.

Always remember to **remove all collars** from the dog when leaving him in the crate.

COLLARS

An appropriate collar is necessary to help control the dog during the training program.

With a young puppy we usually recommend a nylon buckle collar for both training and identification purposes. It should fit around the neck so as not to allow the puppy to pull out of it. Print your pet's name and your phone number directly on the collar.

For stronger, larger dogs or puppies, in addition to a nylon buckle collar, another type of training collar may need to be used.

A professional trainer or other knowledgeable person should be consulted for the correct fitting and utilization of these more specific types of collars, both to avoid injuring the dog and to ensure total effectiveness.

Always remember, **absolutely**, all collars **must** be removed from your dog when he is left alone in the crate for his own safety.

LEASHES

Cotton or leather leashes are easier to grip and gentler on the hands than nylon or chain leashes.

When the puppy or dog is not in the crate, he must be kept on a six foot training leash with you **holding the other end**. At all times? Yes! At all times attached to you, even in the house, when the dog is eating, sleeping, playing, and trying to jump on the furniture or kitchen counters.

This method will enable you to give a training correction immediately when needed and more importantly, keep your dog out of harm's way.

ODOR NEUTRALIZERS

As with any housebreaking program, accidents are bound to happen. Some products are better than others in removing stains and eliminating odors. After removing any solid waste and washing the area, it is important to **neutralize** and **remove** any **trace odor** of urine and feces so that the puppy or dog is not attracted back to the area to urinate or defecate.

A solution of 50% water with 50% white vinegar is an inexpensive yet effective odor neutralizer that we have been using for years. Other excellent products are available commercially. Shop around for the one that works best for you.

OOPS!!

CHAPTER 3

PROPER DIET, FOOD SUPPLEMENTS AND TREATS

Nutrition is an important factor in the health and performance of your dog.

PROPER DIET

There is a direct correlation between what "goes in" to what "comes out." Your choice of dog food is very important. Dog food should contain high quality protein, vitamins, minerals and fiber in amounts necessary for the proper development and maintenance of your individual puppy or dog.

Foods that consist of unnecessary cereal and fiber fillers or excess moisture may only delay your progress by causing the dog to urinate and defecate more frequently.

Individual dogs can vary in the way they metabolize dog food. Pick one food that works for you and stick with it. Avoid sudden dietary changes and additions, because this can change the consistency of the stool and increase the dog's need to defecate. Remember, "If something works, don't fix it!"

As your puppy grows, his intake of food will need to be increased. Do this slowly, in small increments, and you should not experience any adverse effects on housebreaking.

Consult your veterinarian, breeder, trainer, or pet store professional for recommendations on a brand suitable for your specific dog, based on size, age, breed, activity level and any medical condition.

FOOD SUPPLEMENTS

Normal, healthy dogs and puppies that are on a good quality, nutritional dog food should not require additional dietary supplements.

If you *do* use a supplement, realize that certain ones (i.e., oil based coat supplements) can alter the consistency of the stool. And always, consult your veterinarian first, as some food supplements may actually be harmful.

TREATS

Feeding too many treats will create more stool and increase the puppy or dog's need to relieve himself. The type of treats can also affect the consistency and amount of stool. Both of these factors will make it more difficult for the puppy or dog to control himself.

In addition, the puppy may fill up on treats and not consume the necessary amount of his dog food.

We personally recommend an all natural dog biscuit or small pieces of his regular dog food in a limited amount as a treat and teething aid.

CHAPTER 4

METHOD

Keeping control of your puppy or dog at all times during the training process is the most important lesson you must learn.

Whenever the dog or puppy is outside of his crate, he must be attached to a six foot leash with you holding the other end.

Yes! All the time, even in the house, when he is eating, drinking, and playing. By doing this, the dog can never be out of your sight or control. Should the dog start to relieve himself in the house you are in the position to immediately make the proper correction. Quickly snap the leash and at the same time firmly say "NO!" Then take the dog directly outside to his elimination area.

The correction is most effective if given while the dog is in the process of having the "accident." If the leash is not held in your hand, when the dog has an accident you will have to chase after him in order to grab hold of the leash. This will teach the dog to run away from you. And, as a result of anticipating the chase and correction, the dog can become **aggressive or shy**.

When you cannot be attached to your puppy or dog, (i.e.at times when you are gone from the house, or cooking, cleaning, doing laundry, sleeping) he should be in his crate.

Many owners are anxious at the thought of leaving a dog in a crate. Teach your dog to be comfortable in his crate by using an encouraging voice and phrase such as "Kennel up!" each time you place him in it. Initially, provide a treat such as a small piece of natural dog biscuit as an inducement and place safe toys in the crate for his enjoyment. **Never use a crate for punishment!** And always remember to **remove the leash and all collars** after putting him in the crate.

When taking the dog out of the crate, do it calmly and quietly without getting him excited, otherwise he may urinate or develop other problems associated with separation anxiety.

If the puppy or dog should relieve himself in his crate **do not scold him**. Stay calm. Take him out of the crate, clean the mess, use the odor neutralizer, and, if necessary, clean the dog.

If your dog is properly exercised, both mentally and physically, the crate will become a place for rest and security, his "den."

Now that we understand how to control our puppy or dog, we are ready to teach him when and where to relieve himself.

When taking the dog outside for his elimination walk, always use the same door. This will help him identify going out for the specific purpose of voiding. Dress appropriately so that you can comfortably stay outside with your dog. You want him to learn to eliminate during bad as well as good weather.

Choose an area outside that will be used specifically for elimination only. Go directly to this area with the dog on his leash and **stand in one place**. Do not move! By allowing your puppy or dog to investigate or sniff around a larger area, he will become distracted by different sights and scents and not fully concentrate on voiding. Initially leave a small amount of stool down for the puppy to identify "his spot." Keep the remaining area clean. Dogs do not relish stepping in feces any more than you do. This will also help in controlling the spread of intestinal parasites.

Once you have brought the puppy out to the designated elimination area, start repeating in a quiet, monotone voice, a phrase such as "Do your business," "Do your business." (Use this one or make up your own but always use the same phrase). You want the puppy to associate your particular phrase with the actual process of elimination. Later on, this will be helpful in getting the dog to eliminate quickly on command whenever he hears the phrase. Continue repeating the phrase until he starts to void and then be silent while he is urinating or defecating. Wait until he is completely finished and then vocally **praise, praise, praise!** Dogs respond very quickly to your tone of voice, so if you start to praise him during the act he may get distracted and stop.

Allow a **ten minute period** for the dog to relieve himself. Training your dog to **go quickly** when first taken outside will give you control of your valuable time. By taking long walks or playing with the dog before he voids, you are forming a habit that you may not always be able to keep because of weather conditions, illness or time restrictions.

For the first two weeks that you begin the program, you should give the puppy two extra minutes after he has relieved himself to make sure that he has completely finished the process. Many owners rush inside too quickly, only to have the puppy finish inside what he started to do outside.

Once the puppy or dog has relieved himself in the designated area, then it is time for **exercise** and **play.**

If the dog or puppy has not relieved himself within the ten minute time frame, bring him directly back into the house. Don't stay out any longer. Keep him inside until the next scheduled elimination walk. Watch him for any sign that he may need to relieve himself such as circling, smelling the floor, staring at you or pulling towards the door. If so indicated, bring him back outside to the elimination area and repeat the entire process.

Do not, however, try taking him out more frequently than your schedule indicates for an elimination walk if he is not signaling a need to do so, for then he may never learn to control himself for any long period of time.

As your puppy or dog progresses through the training you will become aware of his individual needs and habits and be able to respond appropriately.

Adhere to the housebreaking principles until the dog has had absolutely no "accidents" for a period of at least **twelve consecutive weeks**. Only then would we consider the dog to be housebroken.

CHAPTER 5

SCHEDULE

The schedule we have outlined has accommodated thousands of owners and their dogs.

Follow the basis of this schedule provided for you. It is not written in stone, and may be revised to coincide with your lifestyle, adjusting the times within reason, and to suit your own needs.

Consistency and continuity are essential. Give your initial plan at least five full days to be effective before making any changes.

Those of you who are not available to walk your dog as often as indicated in the schedule, do not fret! Go to work and don't rush home from errands. Dogs will eventually develop enough physical control to become housebroken. If you are gone for more than eight hours, consider hiring a responsible dog walker for at least one midday elimination walk and some playtime, or, arrange for "day care" at a boarding kennel or your veterinarian's office while you are gone.

Scheduling intake of food and water makes it

easier for the dog to control himself. It is more humane than allowing the dog unlimited access to food and water with no chance to urinate or defecate outside. This approach is safe and effective for normal puppies and dogs. If you have any doubts or concerns about managing food and water intake, please consult your veterinarian.

Keep the food down on the floor in front of the dog for a period of fifteen minutes which will allow the dog plenty of time to eat. If the dog does not finish, take up the food until the next scheduled feeding.

Immediately after eating and drinking, dogs should be taken out to eliminate regardless of when they last urinated or defecated. The reason for this is that dogs, like people, after eating or drinking can experience a gastrointestinal reflex with a resultant need to void.

Though not on the schedule provided, there are a few other times that you may want or need to bring your dog or puppy out for an elimination walk:

For puppies under four months of age:
1. Usually after a nap
2. After a snack
3. Before indoor playtime (activity may stimulate the need to void)

For dogs of any age:
Any time indicated by the dog's behavior or signals such as circling, sniffing the floor, pulling toward the door.

EXAMPLE SCHEDULE

TIME	ACTIVITY
7 am	elimination walk play, exercise
8am	food, water, elimination walk play, exercise
11am	water, elimination walk play, exercise
2pm	water, elimination walk play, exercise
5pm	food, water, elimination walk play, exercise
8pm	water, elimination walk play, exercise
11pm	elimination walk

As you see, we have suggested exercise and play frequently in this schedule. This will result in a dog that is calmer in the house and a happier you!

YOUR SCHEDULE

TIME	ACTIVITY

CHAPTER 6

MISCONCEPTIONS

SPITE:

Contrary to what some owners believe, dogs are not spiteful. When they act inappropriately it is because they have not been trained effectively or because of anxiety, fear, stress or illness.

RUB HIS NOSE IN IT:

Based on many years of experience in housebreaking dogs, we find that this way of trying to communicate your displeasure over the dog's mistake is ineffective and may very well cause the development of **aggression and/or shyness** towards you. We strongly advise against this.

CORRECTIONS AFTER THE FACT:

There are some people who conclude that dogs remember old misdeeds and therefore, can be scolded after the fact. This method of correction is rarely effective in teaching the dog not to eliminate in the house.

So many times owners will say that the dog

looks or acts guilty when they return home to find an "accident" in the house. They interpret this to mean that the dog knows he did wrong. What actually is occurring is that the dog knows something is wrong. The owner's negative body language, facial expressions and tone of voice is the cause of the dog's anxiety. The dog is responding simply to what the owner is doing and not to what he has done. Dogs can shy away from you or act "guilty" or fearful after they have relieved themselves in the house, anticipating your anger and punishment.

OLDER DOGS:

Older dogs can and do learn "new tricks," behaviors and commands. Older dogs **can** become housebroken.

You must change what you do if you wish to effect change in your dog. Even if total resolution of the problem is not possible, in most cases acceptable management can be achieved.

RING A BELL:

Many people have asked us to teach their puppy to signal its need to go out to eliminate by ringing a bell or scratching at a door. This is impractical since you may not always be available to respond by letting the dog out. So, what will the dog do? In most cases, if he has been taught with a signal and he gets no response, he will probably tend to void in the house rather than waiting to be let out.

SMALL BREEDS:
There exists a myth that small dogs can't be housebroken. The fact is that they possess as much intelligence and physical ability to become housebroken as any large dog. Owners of small dogs may tend to accept or overlook small accidents for a longer period of time, making it more difficult to effect successful housebreaking.

TWO WEEKS AND TRAINED:
There are people who believe that a dog is housebroken if he has been "clean" in the house for a period of a few weeks. For the most part, what actually happens is that the dog has been good for a couple of weeks and based on this, the owners have given him freedom in the house. The dog begins to have accidents since he was never actually completely housebroken in the first place. The owners control the dog for another few weeks and he's good again so he's given his freedom once more. The same cycle repeats itself over and over, creating a dog that will never be totally housebroken.

We consider a dog to be housebroken only after he has been completely clean in the house for a minimum period of **twelve consecutive weeks**.

POINTS TO REMEMBER

While you must be your dog's teacher you are also the student, still learning and bound to be frustrated at times. Please be patient with yourself and your dog. We strongly encourage you to seek professional advice from your veterinarian or professional dog trainer whenever you feel the need to do so.

We would like to be able to tell you that your dog will be housebroken within a certain period of time. However, the truth is that puppies, like children being "potty trained," are individuals and will become housebroken within varying lengths of time.

Our experience and that of our colleagues indicates that most dogs that are not housebroken are also not very well behaved. Those that are obedient and well behaved tend to be housebroken.

As a result of controlling your puppy for housebreaking purposes, you will be in the best position to also manage other inappropriate behaviors such as jumping up and destructive chewing.

Having the leash in your hand enables you to teach and enforce obedience commands. Obedience training will form a line of communication between you and your dog thus ensuring a long and mutually satisfying relationship.